NFT For

Beginners

A Step-By-Step Guide On How To Create, Sell, And Buy Non-Fungible Tokens To Make Money

Crypto Academy

reader will render any resulting actions solely under their purview. There are no scenarios in which the publisher or the original author of this work can be in any fashion deemed liable for any hardship or damages that may befall them after undertaking information described herein.

Additionally, the information in the following pages is intended only for informational purposes and should thus be thought of as universal. As befitting its nature, it is presented without assurance regarding its prolonged validity or interim quality. Trademarks that are mentioned are done without written consent and can in no way be considered an endorsement from the trademark holder.

Table Of Content

Introduction

Right now, it seems that there isn't anything to talk about but NFTs. The curiosity to understand what they are, why there is so much attention on them, and why they seem to be considered the Holy Grail of investing, seems to have conquered everyone, including you.

I'd say you're definitely in the right place. In this book, we'll explore together everything you need to know if you're a beginner in NFTs.

We'll start by analyzing their meaning, then I'll try to explain to you in the simplest way possible what they are, what applications they will have in the future, and how they will impact your life as a person and as an investor.

You have in your hands a practical guide for beginners that will help you to get a really clear idea of NFTs and really understand the revolution that is happening out there thanks to this new technology. With the information you'll acquire in this book, you can decide whether to be an active part of it by investing in or creating NFTs, or just enjoy their benefits for the foreseeable future.

If you're ready, get comfortable, and let's get going!

What Is An NFT

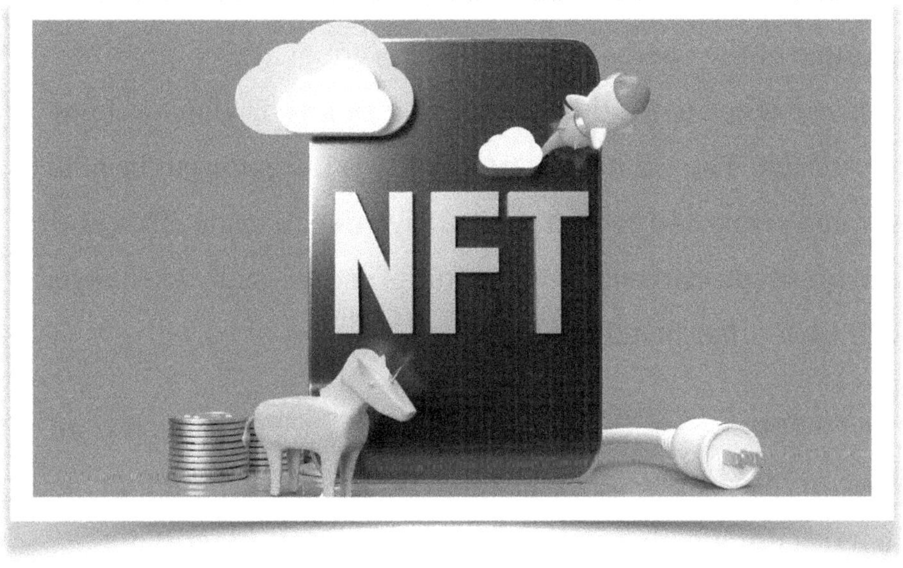

The term NFT stands for Non-Fungible Token.

Fungibility is a quality that is usually attributed to non-unique material goods that are distinguished only by kind and quantity, for example, grain, money, coal. When you make a loan with these goods you only have to pay back the same amount with the same product. For example, if you go to the bank and deposit 10$, then come back to collect them later, it is practically impossible for the cashier to give you back exactly the same bill, but it will still give you back exactly 10$.

Fungible indicates, therefore, that the units of a certain resource are indistinguishable from each other and therefore exchangeable between them. We have already given the example of the 10$ banknote which is equal and compatible with any other 10$ banknote, as long as it is original and not counterfeit. The element of fungibility is necessary to be able to use a resource as a mechanism to give rise to trade. This is also true for cryptocurrencies where units can be easily exchanged with each other just like fiat money.

The NFT, however, is a non-fungible token. Basically, it is an asset, cryptographically registered on the blockchain that includes unique identifying codes and unique identifying information so that each NFT can be distinguished from another. Put in simpler terms, an NFT is a certificate of authenticity or a deed of a specific asset that can be digital or physical. Given their uniqueness, these tokens, which represent a deed or certificate, are not fungible, which means that they cannot be exchanged with each other as can be done with the various cryptocurrencies on the blockchain. Cryptocurrencies are "Fungible Tokens" that are identical to each other and therefore can be exchanged with each other.

Since this is a beginner's manual of NFT, I assume that you are at least familiar with the terms “cryptocurrency" and "blockchain". If not, go to look up the meaning of these two terms because you need to know them to understand what we are talking about now. Here is a brief description.

Simplifying and summarizing as much as possible, cryptocurrencies are digital currencies with a value and can be used as a means of exchange or as a method of investment. The blockchain, on the other hand, is a kind of shared ledger that is impossible to change. This ledger makes it easy to record transactions and track assets, it is very easy to update it with all the necessary data and information, and it does not involve a control and verification unit. Cryptocurrencies and NFTs both use this ledger.

Let's go back to our NFTs and see what their main features are:

- NFTs cannot be duplicated on the blockchain because they are unique cryptographic tokens.

- NFTs can also represent tangible products, not just the digital images you've become accustomed to.

- Creating an NFT of a tangible product serves to make it more efficient. In fact, the NFT largely reduces the risk of fraud or counterfeiting by making the product easier to sell, buy or trade.

- Examples of areas where tangible products can benefit enormously from NFTs are real estate and art. In fact, NFTs can be used to represent the ownership rights that a person has over an asset and also the authenticity of the asset itself. Even the very identity of a person could be represented by an NFT.

As you can tell from this little list, the unique structure of each NFT lends itself to so many different applications. We've mentioned real estate and art in terms of physical products. Selling these products through NFTs would lead to a revolution that, at least in the art world, is already fully underway and it will only take a short while for it to expand to all other possible areas. The use of NFTs completely eliminates the figure of the intermediary, with all that this entails. The artist no longer needs an art gallery, he can reach his potential customers on his own and sell the work linked to an NFT that would certify it as unique and original on the blockchain, attributing ownership to the buyer. The same could apply to a house, creating an NFT token to sell it would automatically register the deed on the blockchain ledger, leaving out intermediaries and bureaucracy.

I mentioned that art has already been fully invested in this phenomenon, particularly digital art. The artist Beeple created a collage with images of his first 5000 days of work, made an NFT out of it, and sold it on auction for $69 million. Beeple with his work has set a new record for the most expensive piece of digital art ever sold through an auction.

In this last period, we are witnessing a real boom of digital collectibles turned into NFT that are making sales with numbers that seem incredible.

At the moment, the largest slice of the NFT market is represented by digital artwork, sports cards, digital photography, various rarities, and gaming items inside famous video games. The famous Top Shot company, known worldwide for its collectible physical sports cards, has created an NFT collection of digital NBA cards. Some of these cards have been auctioned off online for millions of dollars.

The founder of the social network Twitter, who is also a digital entrepreneur, created an NFT of his first post on Twitter. This NFT was auctioned off online for two and a half million dollars.

If you give another look to the amounts paid by collectors to secure a rare NFT in their collection, you should begin to understand that all this big money moving around thanks to this technology, has generated all the hype surrounding NFTs and why almost everyone is talking about them.

Difference Between Cryptocurrencies And NFTs

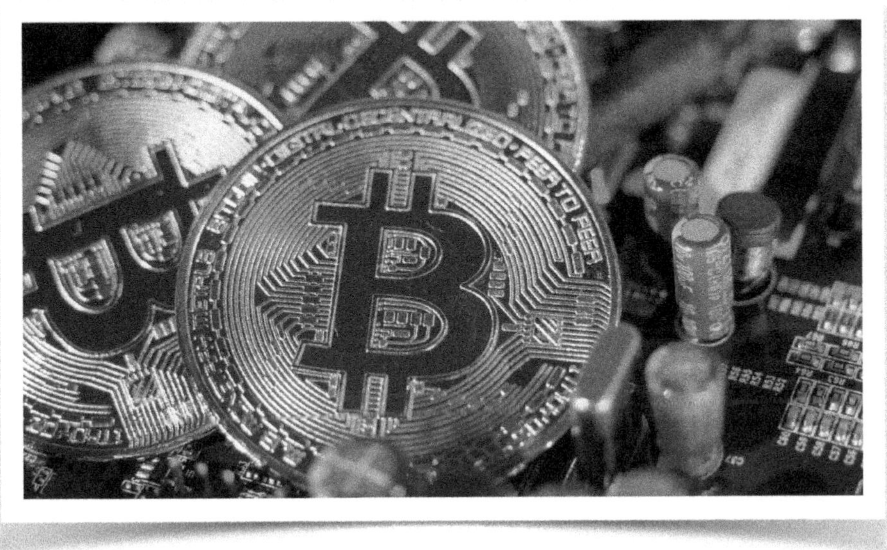

Just like tangible currencies technically called fiat currencies, i.e. the banknotes you use every day, digital currencies can also be spent or exchanged for other currencies. A Dollar is worth exactly the same as another Dollar and, similarly, a Bitcoin is worth exactly the same as another Bitcoin or an Ethereum is worth the same as another Ethereum. You can spend your Dollar or you can exchange its value for an equivalent amount of Pounds just as you can spend your Bitcoin or exchange it for an equivalent amount of Ethereum. These are all fungible currencies.

With NFTs, you have to make a total paradigm shift because of their uniqueness. As each NFT is unique, different from any other, and impossible to replace, no two NFTs can in any way be compared to each other, and therefore two NFTs never have the same value and one cannot be worth as much as the other.

This is exactly what "non-fungible token" means, as we discussed in the previous chapter. An NFT is a cryptographic token that gives a product uniqueness, identity, authenticity decreeing that it is good and true, and also traceability that allows us to monitor who is the owner and how much they paid for it. Through these characteristics, its market value is established.

We could compare the NFT to a digital passport, in fact, each token has its own non-transferable identity that allows it to distinguish itself from any other token. NFTs are represented by a digital image that corresponds to an asset or resource. The interesting element is that 2 NFTs can be combined to generate a third one.

Technically an NFT can contain any digital file and the blockchain keeps track of the person that owns the file at that moment, plus it tracks all the previous owners so you can trace its history backward.

A common element between NFTs and cryptocurrencies is that both provide ownership data that makes it straightforward to recognize a given token and, consequently, to transfer it from one owner to another.

In the case of the NFT, however, the owner can add additional information or special features related to the NFT itself. Let me give an example in the field of art. In the case of a piece of digital artwork, the artist could decide to add his autograph to the metadata and make it part of the NFT created for that artwork.

NFTs are born from the ERC-721 standard. The acronym stands for Ethereum Request For Comments 721, it is basically a Smart Contract with an API inside. This structure gives NFTs the fantastic features we have already discussed: namely uniqueness, different value than another token, and transferability from one account to another.

If you are wondering what a Smart Contract is, it is a program that runs on the blockchain, in the case of NFTs mainly on the Ethereum blockchain. It is mainly through this Cryptocurrency that it is possible to buy, create and invest in NFTs, but we will deal with this topic in more detail in one of the next chapters.

So, the NFT is not really a cryptocurrency, as people tend to believe, but a product of it. We have already mentioned that an NFT can be a work of art or a collector's item, but if you understand all the incredible implications it has, it can also be used to generate access keys, lottery tickets, or tickets for sporting events or concerts and much more.

We have already pointed out that the main difference between cryptocurrencies and NFTs is the uniqueness of NFTs and the fact that this uniqueness gives a different value to each NFT. The value can be determined by its rarity, its age, the community or services it allows you to access, and also by its appearance.

The first ERC-721 created (that is the first NFT) is a clear example of value related to appearance and rarity and I'm sure you have already heard of it. I am referring to Cryptokitties, the game created in November 2017 where you are the owner of a virtual kitten that you have to take care of, you have to feed, and raise. Each digital representation of a kitten in the game has a unique identification on the Ethereum blockchain. Each kitten is unique and has a corresponding monetary value expressed in Ethereum.

If you remember, we previously mentioned that two NFTs can generate a third. Well, back to our game, by owning two virtual kittens you can make them generate a puppy, which will be unique, with characteristics and value different from that of its "parents".

To talk a bit about stratospheric numbers and get an idea of the reach and impact that NFT has and will have on an ever-increasing scale, fans of the game have spent the equivalent of $20 million in Ethereum, just a few weeks after launch to buy their kittens, feed them and take care of them. The most passionate players have spent more than $100,000 on their crypto kitten.

For many, the use made of NFT technology in Cryptokitties is insignificant, but the focus should be on the commercial ramifications that this technology can have. Just think of the real estate transactions we mentioned earlier or the private equity transactions that could be made. The revolution is already underway and we need to be part of it.

Why NFTs Are So Important

NFTs are a big step forward in the relatively simple and straightforward concept of cryptocurrencies. Modern financial systems involve complex exchanges and lending systems for a very wide range of categories such as loan contracts, real estate, art and so much more. NFTs will take all this a step further and they will simplify it because they will generate digital representations of physical assets and this will bring a wide range of benefits.

The concept of a digital representation of a physical asset and the concept of using unique identification are not new concepts. The big force that will drive the change is hooking these old concepts into smart contracts on the blockchain.

Converting a physical asset into a digital asset greatly simplifies the transactions related to that asset and also eliminates most of the middlemen. This market efficiency is probably the benefit that first comes to mind when we talk about NFT.

We have already said that, in the artistic field, a digital-only work or even a physical one represented with an NFT on the blockchain can be sold directly by the artist, there is no need for an art gallery or another intermediary, the artist is in direct contact with his final consumer. But this concept is very valid for a lot of other businesses and allows them to improve their procedures and performances. Think, for example, of an NFT of a rare, valuable, and expensive bottle of wine. It is easy to interact with its path for anyone interested. You can identify with certainty its provenance, who produced it, and, finally, you can make the purchase. (Obviously, you'll have your image of the bottle connected to the registration on the blockchain and then you'll receive the physical bottle associated with it).

Also, think about how useful NFTs can be for managing personal identities. When you travel you always have to show your passport, follow procedures to check for its authenticity. Turning your passport into an NFT would make everything easier. There would be no risk of fake documents and fake identities. Unique and distinctive qualities of the passport's owner could easily be included and easily updated at any time, with a precise record of each update and variations done. This would also solve the problem of digital identities, thus simplifying online bureaucracy. The need for requesting documents online is becoming more and more frequent, but proving one's digital identity keeps becoming harder because of all the online frauds happening. With an NFT it would be easy and safe.

Turning a physical asset into a digital one also makes it much easier to invest in that asset with other people. A piece of land, an apartment, or a work of art can have more than one owner. Turning any of these assets into an NFT makes it much easier to split up each asset precisely so that several people can own a small portion each, and that portion measures exactly the same amount for each investor. This simplification brings many investments within reach of a larger number of users.

These new investment opportunities and the new markets that NFTs open up for investment are the most interesting and appealing aspects of NFTs for most people. You can invest in digital art, you can buy and sell land in the metaverse, and even trade assets within video games, such as avatars, collectibles, domains, and more.

Being on the same blockchain as cryptocurrencies, NFTs represent pretty safe investments, in fact, they are very difficult (though not impossible) to hack. The biggest security issue is the platform on which they are held. If the platform shuts down, you might no longer be able to access your NFTs.

Key Features Of An NFT

Incredibly Extraordinary:

Just as in the cases of great works of art, in digital art duplicates of works are also frequent. While in classical art it is almost impossible to distinguish the original from the copies made later, with NFTs the true and sole owner of the first work can claim it without a doubt, thanks to its traceability on the blockchain. A copy of work can also be widely shared on the network, and usually, it is, but the true owner can always claim it without a shadow of a doubt.

It Is Not Inter-Operable:

An NFT of a kitten from Cryptokitties cannot be used in Decentraland or vice versa. The same applies to in-game items or collectible cards belonging to different games.

Determined:

Unlike cryptocurrency, NFTs cannot be divided or separated into smaller or modest pieces.

Indestructible:

All the information about an NFT is written on the blockchain, so the token cannot be deleted, removed or taken off the blockchain, or even reproduced. The liability on the token produced is also permanent, so the token belongs to its owner and not the person who produces it. For example, if you buy an ebook on Amazon you are not claiming the book as your own, you are buying permission to read it whenever you want.

Indubitable:

The blockchain records and keeps in memory every change in ownership of the NFT in chronological order. This allows you to walk back through the history of that NFT from its creation to the last current owner, along with the prices paid at each stage of the exchange.

Full Ownership:

Thanks to the indubitable proof given by the blockchain ledger that that asset is yours, you can prove full ownership even if it's something that seems elusive or easily replicated.

Where To Buy NFTs

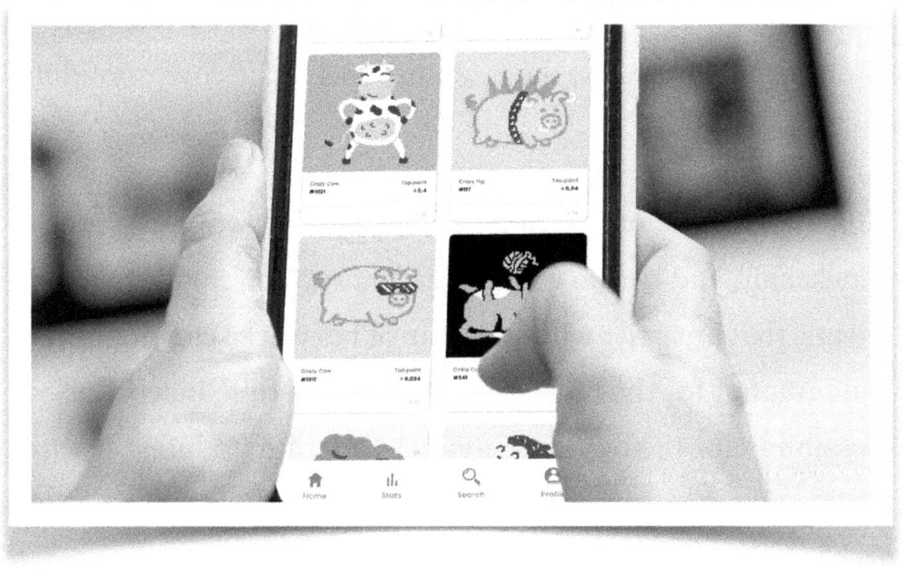

Many people think it is illogical and a bit crazy to spend millions of dollars, or even just a few hundreds, to buy a GIF or computer graphics file. On the other hand, there are plenty of other people who can't wait to pay these sums of money to secure ownership of something they could just look at or take a screenshot of and keep a copy of. Did you ever wonder why?

The reason is that NFTs are so much more than those little images you think you're buying. NFTs create a direct link between financial and social capital because each one gives access and participation to its own community, creating networks and links between individuals. So, when you buy your little image, you are also buying access to these groups of individuals and the more these groups include exclusive or prominent characters, the more expensive the corresponding NFTs will be.

The information of each NFT is immutably recorded on the blockchain and has an authentication system built into it. This means that an artist who sells one of his works can digitally autograph it for the buyer and at the same time insert the possibility for the buyer to interact with him, to interact with the artist and creator himself, to become part of his community and to be able to show others all the works in his possession created by that same artist.

A person that owns some particular NFTs (unique ones, expensive ones, ones that include very exclusive benefits, and so on) and that shows them and his certified ownership gains a certain social status. So, when you invest in NFTs you also invest in securing that high social status. Having and showing these works in the digital world gives the owner a big social boost, allowing him to create connections and bonds that strengthen him and continuously increase his social status in the eyes of those who look at his collection.

Contributing to this particularly high social status is the fact that NFTs are unique, a key feature in the world of serious collecting. For example, a digital image may have been shared countless times, but only one will own the NFT of that image, with all the impact this uniqueness brings to the collector's image and social status. Who wouldn't want to form relationships with someone who owns so many expensive rarities?

I'd like to point out that when you purchase an NFT you don't purchase copyright, that remains with the person creating the content. You buy a token that connects on the blockchain your identity to the piece of art purchased. This is the most valuable element for the buyer, the fact that the NFT declares that the collector owns the original product registered on the blockchain and whose image serves as proof of ownership.

If you're now wondering where you can go to buy your first NFT to enter this revolutionary world, get comfortable because there's a lot to say.

There are plenty of online marketplaces where you can buy and trade NFTs. They don't all work the same way, they don't all have the same types of NFTs, and they don't all have the same features.

The vast majority of platforms use the Ethereum blockchain, but many provide non-Ethereum-based NFT services. I'll list 3 of the most popular non-Ethereum-based at the time I'm writing this book:

1. Cosmos

2. Binance Smart Chain

3. Polkadot

I won't say more about them because this is a beginner's guide and it is a lot easier for beginners to start out in the biggest NFT market, which, at the moment, is the Ethereum-based blockchain. Those "side-markets" exist, but you should explore them once your level of knowledge and awareness of this world is wider and deeper.

So, the "major" NFTs marketplaces are based on Ethereum, and we are going to analyze the distinctions, weaknesses, and strengths of the best ones, at the moment I am writing this guide.

The distinctions between the various marketplaces carry as much importance for those who create and distribute NFT as they do for those who purchase it. These differentiators may be the types of files accepted by the platform, the accessibility of the platform, the cost to create an NFT, and other such aspects for those who create and distribute. On the other hand, for buyers, the differentiators may be the security of the marketplace, its reliability, or its ease of use.

Although each of these marketplaces operates differently, most of them still offer a fairly wide range of NFT types for sale. What differentiates a casual investor from an experienced one, however, is choosing the marketplace based on the type of NFTs that you want to acquire or create or invest in. Once you have decided on the type of NFT you want, you need to look for the best marketplace for that type of token.

At the time of writing this book, 10 marketplaces are considered the top for buying, creating, and trading NFTs. I'll list them for you and then we'll go over a few details for each one together:

1. OpenSea
2. Larva Labs
3. Axie Infinity Marketplace
4. Rarible
5. NBA Top Shot Marketplace
6. SuperRare
7. Nifty Gateway

8. Foundation

9. Theta Drop

10. Mintable

OpenSea

OpenSea is the marketplace that is considered the market leader for selling and buying NFTs. This platform offers a wide range of digital materials in many different categories: photos, music, art, and much more. You can register for free and have a look at everything available for sale in their marketplace.

It's also an interesting platform for those who want to create and sell their own NFTs, as it allows creators to do so with a simple approach and gives great support to all kinds of artists and creators. In technical jargon, creating your own NFT is called "Minting".

If you're new to the world of NFTs, OpenSea is probably the best place to start because of the width of options available and also because it accepts payments in over 150 different cryptocurrencies.

Larva Labs

This marketplace is mainly known for an NFT project that went viral a few years ago called "CryptoPunks".

In 2017, CryptoPunks were given away for free, but over the years the owners that got them for free resold their CryptoPunks, and some of them made millions of dollars. Larva Lab continues to work on many other digital art and app development projects based on the Ethereum blockchain, but the CryptoPunks have long since sold out. They can currently only be purchased at auction on third-party marketplaces.

However, there are also a number of their initiatives that are worth following and keeping an eye on in their marketplace including, at the moment, the "Meebits".

Axie Infinity Marketplace

Axie Infinity is a video game where legendary animals called Axies fight each other to win prizes. The Axie Marketplace is an online store where a player buys his animal, trains it, and prepares it for battle. In the store, besides the Axies, it is possible to buy land and items to use in the game. Obviously, everything you buy is an NFT.

The creators of the game have created a cryptocurrency based on Ethereum called Axie Shards that allows you to give players a series of rewards and incentives. The Axis Shards cryptocurrency can be found on many other NFT marketplaces, but also on a cryptocurrency exchange, such as CoinBase.

Rarible

Rarible is a marketplace very similar to OpenSea that manages a very wide range of NFTs. You can create, buy, sell and trade NFTs in the form of art, music, collectibles, and movies.

The key difference with OpenSea is that to buy or sell on the Rarible marketplace you have to use their cryptocurrency, the Rarible token, which is based on the Ethereum blockchain.

You can also buy some of their artworks on OpenSea, but the means of payment is still their Rarible token.

This marketplace has gained its importance thanks to the numerous initiatives shared with famous companies. Adobe, the great software, and digital company joined Rarible to help NFT artists and creators safeguard their work. Taco Bell has created and posted labeled artwork on the platform.

NBA Top Shot Marketplace

NBA's men and women have entered the NFT world thanks to Top Shot. You used to collect stickers of your favorite players with different degrees of rarity, now you can collect moments in the form of NFT. Now you can buy video clips, highlights, and pieces of art from the most famous basketball league in the world, directly from their marketplace.

Their marketplace is closed, you can only buy and sell Top Shot NFTs. The registration process is simple and you can buy something for just a few dollars.

SuperRare

SuperRare is very similar to Rarible. It is a marketplace for digital products in form of NFTs, where you can buy artwork such as 3d images, movies or paintings, paying in Ethereum.

SuperRare artworks, like those of Rarible, can also be bought and traded on OpenSea.

SuperRare recently launched an Ethereum-based cryptocurrency that bears the same name as the marketplace. These tokens will be used to discover and launch new talented artists on the platform.

Nifty Gateway

Nifty Gateway, in addition to being a platform where you can create and sell NFTs, is a platform where you can hold them. In fact, what you buy on Nifty is not held in your wallet, but is held on the Nifty Gateway platform.

This is not exactly ideal for those who invest in NFTs. Usually, these investors prefer much more flexibility in their investments. However, it must be said that this platform offers a great advantage for less experienced investors. Purchases and sales can be made in fiat currencies (e.g. dollars or euros), i.e. without buying cryptocurrencies first.

Many successful artists have sold their works through Nifty Gateway including Beeple for visual art and Grimes for music. This art exchange platform is curated and created by the Winklevoss brothers.

Foundation

Foundation was created to be a fast, straightforward, no-nonsense way to auction digital art. Sales are made in Ethereum and since its launch in 2021 at the time of this writing the platform has sold NFTs for more than $100 million.

Again, all you need is a wallet with Ethereum to make purchases. It's a great marketplace and even artists are invited to join, although it's not the easiest and fastest option if you're just starting out as an NFT creator. A lot of artwork is available and it's pretty easy to browse.

Tetha Drop

Theta started as a decentralized platform on the blockchain for video and television distribution over the internet. In 2021 Theta debuted its NFT store, Theta Drop, where digital artifacts related to the World Poker Tour are sold. The World Poker Tour Series was an early adopter of ThetaTV by streaming its programs on the network.

You can only participate in the purchase when the NFTs are dropped (released) and to participate you must first purchase Theta Token, their cryptocurrency which is supported by many cryptocurrency exchanges.

You have the choice to save the NFTs purchased with Tetha into your crypto wallet or into your Theta wallet.

Mintable

Mintable was founded by billionaire Mark Cuban. Its purpose is to create a marketplace similar to OpenSea.

To buy and sell NFTs on Mintable you must first purchase Ethereum. To participate in Mintable's activities you will need to buy Ethereum on an exchanger platform (like CoinBase), then create a digital wallet to hold your cryptocurrencies, and then connect this wallet to Mintable (actually this is the method you use for most marketplaces, but we will discuss that in details later on).

The platform allows creators and artists of all kinds to create NFTs and then put them on the market, we are talking about musicians, photographers, 3d graphic designers, filmmakers, and so on.

The NFTs you buy, in most cases, are stored in a virtual wallet on the platform, where you can also watch your collection. You can also transfer them to an external wallet, even though not all wallets are accepted.

This is how a wallet usually looks like:

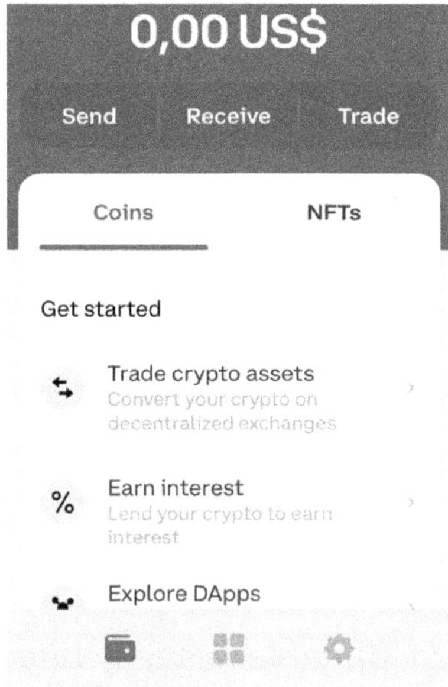

The most reliable and popular wallets at the time of writing this book are:

- Metamask
- Coinbase Wallet
- Math Wallet
- Alpha Wallet
- Trust Wallet

You will be able to sell or trade your NFTs on most of the marketplaces we have seen so far, with related features. At the moment OpenSea is considered the main one. The purpose of these marketplaces is simply to associate buyers and sellers in order to create commercial transactions. For each transaction of the same NFT, the estimate of its value changes. Usually, what determines the value is the interest of the marketplace in a particular NFT, either because of the aesthetic aspect or because of the community that the NFT can give you access to. For this reason, in most cases, for the most requested NFTs, you need to participate in an auction to get them.

The purchase/sale transaction is recorded immediately on the blockchain and the payment in the concerned cryptocurrency takes place immediately and without any possibility of error. At the exact moment the transaction takes place, a permanent record is made on the blockchain of the purchase providing proof of ownership.

The question I usually get at this point is: "Is it possible to make money by buying NFT?". The answer is "Yes, but ...".

As for cryptocurrencies, the fast price fluctuation allows you to make a lot of money quickly, but lose it just as quickly, if you don't know what you are doing. It is important to study an NFT project thoroughly before putting your money into it. The hype on this topic at the moment is very high and this means that there are many people out there with not entirely honest intentions who sponsor unworthy projects for their own personal advantage. The keyword here is “CAUTION”! It's nice to be among the first to get in on the new trends, but the first stages are the ones where you have to pay extra attention.

It is different if you are buying as a collector and not to make money. In that case, you can buy what you like within the limits of your possibilities and show the world your wonderful collection.

Another way to make money with NFT is to create and sell your own works of art. We will see this option in detail later on, but it gives you the possibility to make some money without risking big money or scams.

NFTs And Digital Art

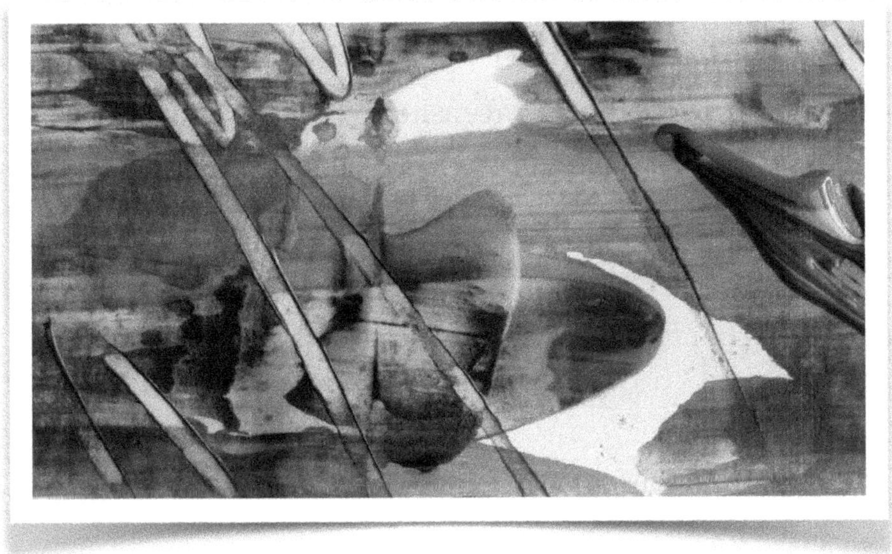

Crypto art, i.e. digital artworks, are currently the ones that exploit NFT technology the most. Digital artwork is associated with a unique token making it unique in turn and guaranteeing its originality. So now the work of art has become an NFT.

To give value to crypto art is the concept of rarity that is at the base of the concept of NFT, the fact that the piece is unique or, at least, the quantity is extremely limited. This concept of scarcity linked to a digital good means that the digital good is compared to a physical good, with the consequent possibility to speculate on the price of the product based on its rarity, uniqueness, and differentiating characteristic. Let me explain.

A photo, a digital postcard, or a video, or music clip can be saved millions of times through screenshots or various download systems. The moment that video, photo, song, or drawing is associated with an NFT, that one will become The One, true and unique. Only the lucky owner will be able to display the original in his collection because he will own the code of registration on the blockchain.

Think about the Cryptokitties game we talked about earlier on. Your cat is unique and you are the one and only lucky owner. Think about the collector who bought the Beeple picture we mentioned earlier. Only one lucky owner holds the original (even though online there are millions of photos of that image) with all that that entails in terms of social status to have it in the collection, given the staggering amount of money at which it was purchased.

If you are an artist, physical or digital, bringing your art to the blockchain could be a useful and important step for your artistic future and this could be the best moment to make this big step. Not only could selling your art in the form of NFTs bring you revenue, but at the same time, it will help you protect your artwork, track all the buying and selling phases and have a clear, accurate, and unalterable record of everything you've produced.

I think it's pretty easy to see why the idea of selling art in all its forms through NFT can not only work, it's already doing quite well and is destined to get even better.

Collecting objects is one of the oldest and most common hobbies in the world and among the most classic collected objects I can think of stamps, coins, and Baseball players' cards, to mention an example dear to young readers, but also to less young ones. At a more refined and expensive level, surrounding oneself with works of art is also part of collecting, and this is the reason why they are called art collections. The common and basic element is always exclusivity. Whether it is a unique sculpture, a rare painting, a much sought-after old figurine, or a stamp that has almost disappeared from the market. It is the scarcity, uniqueness, and rarity that give value.

This is the reason why people spend a lot of money to buy a work of art or a unique collector's item. Until not long ago it was impossible to transfer this characteristic to the digital world, but now, thanks to NFTs, it is possible.

Digital products are, by their very nature, available to everyone, easy to copy, and therefore lacking in uniqueness. NFTs solve this problem so that artists and craftsmen can bring their art into the digital world safely and with great satisfaction. VIPs of all art forms have also become very enthusiastic about this phenomenon because, thanks to it, they can interact directly with their fans, continuing to expand their popularity, and incrementing the number of people consuming their products.

In addition to Beeple, another piece of art sold at an attractive price was the 3D sculpture attributed to the artist who works under the pseudonym Pak. The sculpture is called "Metarift" and is actually a looped video with reflective spheres forming the infinity symbol. At first glance, it may look like a simple animated GIF of which the web is full, but this has been made unique and non-fungible, it has been transformed into NFT, it has been registered on the blockchain with its unique registration code. The perceived value of this artwork was quite high and it has been sold for just under $905,000.

Another highly sought-after artist in the NFT world is Kevin Abosh. To him, we can attribute at least two millionaire creations. The first work, "Forever rose", represents a beautiful red rose on a black background. An immortal rose, transformed into NFT and made unique, sold for 1 million dollars. Certainly, an impactful Valentine's Day gift as it is unique and special. The second work of the artist was a photo of a potato minted into an NFT. The name of the work is "The Potato" and it was sold to an entrepreneur for 1 million dollars.

NFTs are not only used by artists in the visual arts world, but also by celebrities in other fields such as music. In the music world, to name one, rapper Snoop Dogg has created an NFT tied to an original song, created specifically for the NFT, and titled precisely "NFT". The project includes for the buyer a photographic journey through the history of the singer starting from his early career, the tune itself, and also some artwork.

Another interesting example is that of skater Tony Hawk. He created an NFT of the video of himself performing his latest 540° Ollie (a special stunt on a skateboard). In addition to the uniqueness given by the minting of the video into NFT, those who buy it will have the footage of the last performance of this stunt by the champion and this makes it doubly special and unique.

Singer Lindsay Lohan has launched a new single, the song "Fans Forever". The song can be heard on virtually all streaming platforms, but the version converted to NFT was wrapped in an exclusive package and sold for a whopping $50,000.

Rob Gronkowski, NFL celebrity and 4-time Super Bowl champion, launched a series of trading cards in the form of NFTs that netted him $1.6 million in total.

Even NBA star Denis Rodman entered the NFT world by selling 10 NFTs of photos coming from his personal collection, never published before photos, which made him a fair bit of money.

It's clear that digital art in the form of NFT has no limits. It ranges from images to videos, to music, to trading cards, and much more, including the most diverse combinations of two or more individual elements. I think it's safe to say that the only limit is in the mind of the creator. Money doesn't seem to be a limit either, the earnings already made by many artists have proven to be virtually limitless.

The 2 Main Advantages Of Crypto Art

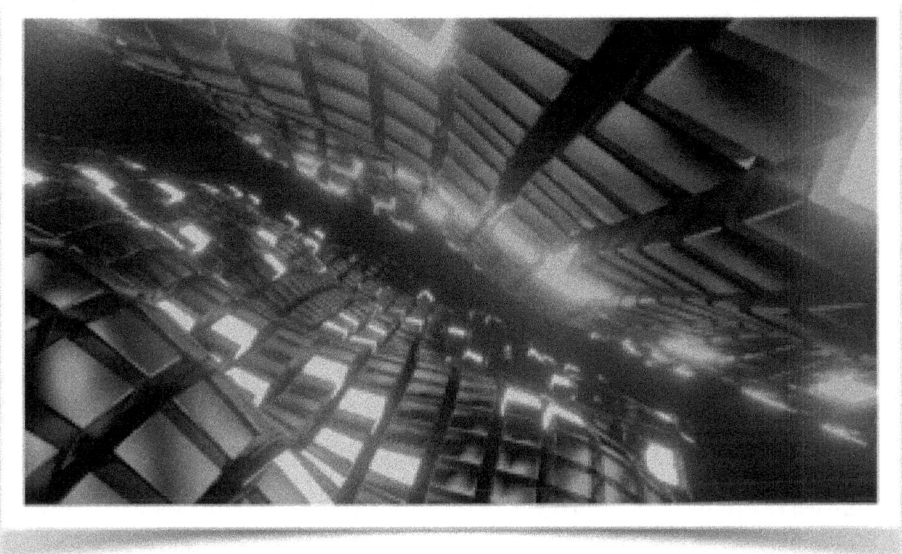

By crypto art, I mean what I described in the previous chapter: a meeting between art, technology, and money. This art form has two main advantages, both very important to understand and know for those who want to invest in NFT crypto art and also for artists who want to enter this world.

We've mentioned the first one before, but it deserves a closer look. Artists and art collectors can meet directly without the need for intermediaries. An artist can sell his NFT work directly, without the need for intermediaries like galleries and auction houses. This innovation gives artists more control over their work, how they distribute it, and how much profit they make from it. At the same time, it allows buyers to have easier access to their favorite artist's work, and at a more affordable price, since all transactions take place online and not in person, eliminating the middleman percentage.

The benefit is obvious for both parties because the artist is the complete custodian of his work until the moment of sale and has total freedom to charge as much as he wants, while the buyer can buy the work directly from the artist, whenever he wants without having to worry about intermediary costs.

The second advantage of artistic NFTs is that they are considered an important part of the crypto economy. They are considered a sort of bridge between cryptocurrencies and fiat money (normal circulating money). Your NFT is digital proof that you are for all intents and purposes the owner of a certain work. That NFT work, unlike physical work, is very easy to transfer to another owner, as there is no need for intermediaries such as galleries or auction houses. This makes NFTs extremely liquid. Given market and technology trends, and the speed at which they are moving, it could even be predicted that in the near future NFTs could become collateral assets, to be used as collateral for a loan or mortgage.

The future of art-related NFTs certainly looks very bright. The key factor in these bright predictions is certainly the popularity that blockchain technology is gaining, and at an astonishing speed. Moreover, this popularity is not limited to niche groups or sub-cultures, it is a real social phenomenon that includes the most diverse age groups.

NFT crypto art collecting even seems to be more successful than traditional art collecting, probably because it is easier to get an original piece at a reasonable price. In addition, NFTs have an aesthetic as well as an economic value, something that some forms of traditional art do not have.

In addition, there are many experts in the physical art market who predict that this fusion of art and technology has every intention of staying and generating a thriving and growing market. Some of these experts even go so far as to advise the various artistic exponents not to close themselves off to the phenomenon, but rather to open themselves up to the creation of NFTs.

Obviously, these are momentary evaluations and predictions, what you need to evaluate is if crypto art can be an interesting investment for you, in light of what you have read and will read in the next pages.

The Most Interesting NFTs Projects

Art

We have already widely discussed and repeated how art represents one of the most interesting projects in the NFT world, both for those who want to start investing in this new world and for artists of all kinds, who want to expand their market with this new incredible technology.

We have already mentioned, in a previous chapter, some of the many marketplaces where it is possible to create, sell and buy NFT crypto art.

The artistic taste and criteria of each collector are different, but the material on the platforms is vast enough to satisfy the tastes, requirements, and wallets of all categories of users.

One project that I found very interesting is Art Block. It is a generative digital art platform with an interesting feature. The collector buys his NFT without knowing in advance what he will get. The artist writes a code that is inserted in the platform, and this code generates variants, and random combinations, whose final result will be your NFT.

Another interesting element of the project, in addition to the unpredictability of the work purchased, is that, in order to purchase a work, you have to participate in a drop. The drop of an item means that you have to wait for the launch of a project and participate in something similar to a draw to be able to purchase what you want (those who buy or collect snackers are certainly familiar with the concept).

When the project of a certain artist is announced, the buyer will go to the page and try to buy his NFT, without knowing what it will look like. Kind of like the surprise bags we used to get at kids at the newsstand, which always had a surprising appeal.

Finally, another art project that I find interesting is Hashmasks. Hashmasks are digital portraits. By purchasing them and holding your purchase every day you accumulate tokens of their cryptocurrency (NCT - NameChanger Token) and that coin will allow you to give a unique name to the artwork you purchased, and to write the name you chose on the Ethereum blockchain. Yet another proof that the strength of NFTs is the uniqueness that they can provide, and that is reflected in the status of those who own those uniquenesses.

Collectibles

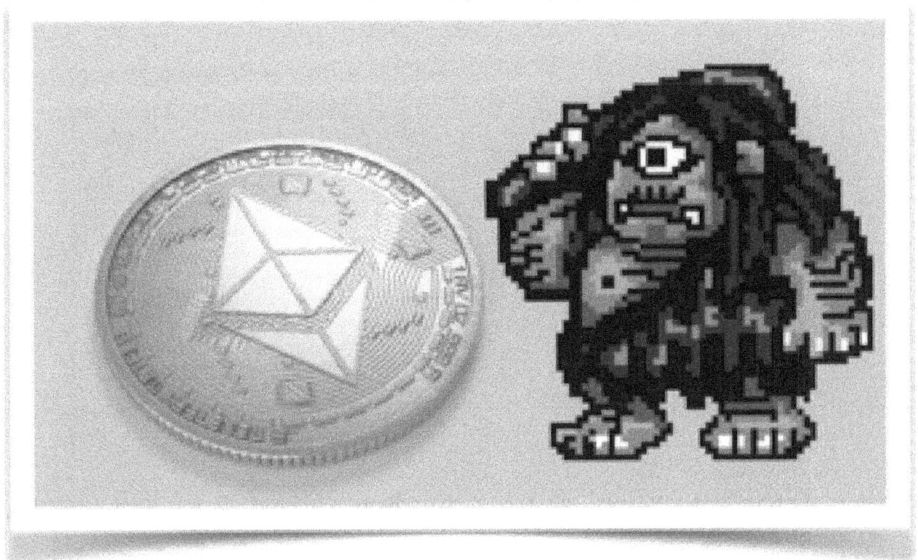

Collectibles have also been discussed before in the book, in the sense that art is also collectible and that many collectibles are also real works of art.

The main marketplaces for purchases, exchanges, creation, and sale of collectibles are always the same as described so far.

There are many interesting projects, and some of them we have already described such as the CryptoPunks. You could go on the various marketplaces and have a look at each project to get a clear idea of what are the best ones, evaluate which ones to invest in, or get inspired to start creating your own NFTs.

We mentioned CryptoPunks, but also MeeBits both from the same manufacturer. Other projects that I personally find interesting are:

- Prime Ape Planet PAP
- Bears Deluxe
- Birdez Gang
- Crazy Fury

You can find these projects on OpenSea and what makes them interesting, in my opinion, in addition to the pretty pictures to collect, are the projects behind each group of "digital collectible cards”. I am talking about the incredible community of which you become in some way part by owning your bird, your monkey, your bear, or your ping-pong racket.

Other interesting projects in the area of collectibles are also related to the world of gaming. We mentioned CryptoKitties earlier, but interesting and noteworthy is the Aavegotchi project. Does anyone remember the Tamagotchi? It was a computerized pet that you always carried with you in a small keychain with a liquid crystal screen, and that you had to take care of: feed, play, clean ... The Aavegotchis are the NFT and futuristic version of the famous pet of the 90s. You buy your own unique NFT pet, give it a unique name, and as you care for it, you make it acquire points and characteristics that make it increasingly rare.

Games are an easy way to take your first steps into the world of NFT, but they can be quite "addictive". I say this because almost everything you do in these games is paid in digital currencies and, therefore it is, in my opinion, a kind of investment. It may be right to do it and you certainly get pleasure from it, but I think it should be done with due awareness.

Another nice example of collectibles is memes. There are millions of them on the web. The most famous one to mention is "Doge". The Shiba Inu symbol of the cryptocurrency Dogecoin is a meme that populates the web. The original meme, minted into an NFT, was sold for one million seven hundred thousand dollars. Certainly, an interesting object to collect, even more so because the cryptocurrency to which it is inspired, at the time, has not reached even a dollar value per token.

Real Estate with Virtual Land

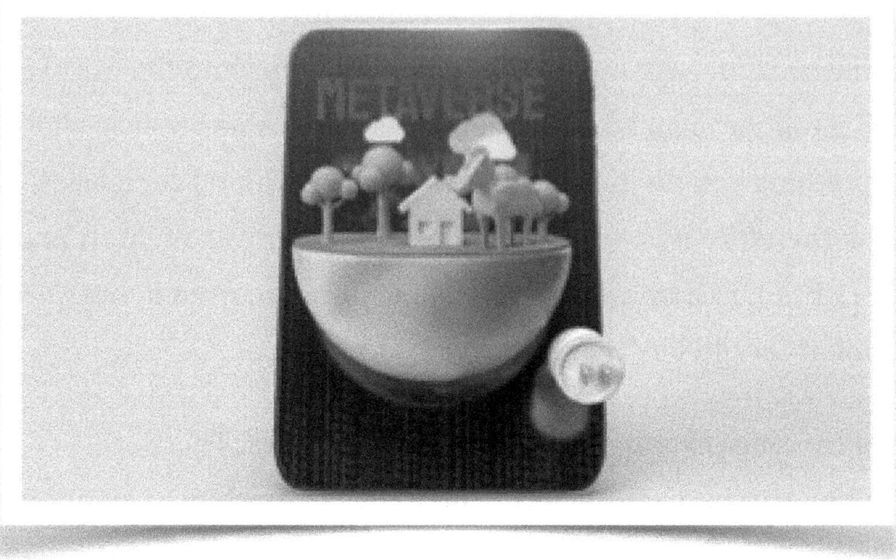

NFTs are also used to build virtual land blocks in the metaverse and for real estate-related objects, e.g. stores, houses, shopping centers, and so on. This is another interesting project that is gathering a lot of investors curious to discover this new virtual world. The subject of the metaverse and its real estate properties and solutions is too vast to be dealt with here, I will deal with it in a separate book. However, I could not avoid introducing it because virtual real estate is, to all intents and purposes, an NFT that can be bought and sold with the procedures that we will analyze later.

You can choose to buy land or virtual real estate directly from the platforms of the various projects. It is a rather safe and appropriate procedure if you have first done the necessary research to understand if the platform is authentic and trustworthy. If you are unsure, marketplaces are always the safest option. For example, on OpenSea you can find all the major NFT projects related to virtual real estate, and make your purchases with more confidence.

Using a marketplace with a good reputation has also an additional advantage: it allows you to get some important information to evaluate a purchase, in fact, you can see the level of interest that the market has towards that project and establish if the asking price seems correct according to the market demand, but also to see that it is not a fraud.

The two projects that are making record takings in this field are:

- The Sandbox
- Decentraland

There are a few other projects that are gaining a good deal of interest at the moment I'm writing this chapter and they are:

- CryptoVoxels
- Somnium Space
- SuperWorld

The Sandbox is a video game that takes place in a virtual metaverse where you have your own avatar and, to be able to play, you buy land, you build on it, and this land will then be yours with the unique and special characteristics that you have given it. You can also buy game items, everything else you buy in the game is an NFT as well.

Decentraland is a video game too. A virtual 3D world where you can buy virtual plots of land and build on them. It is an ever-changing virtual world where the owners are the players, in fact, each player owns his own avatar, his accessories, his land, and so on, all in the form of NFTs.

Each project charges whatever you get within the game with its own cryptocurrency, MANA for Decentraland and SAND for The Sandbox, for example.

We are talking about video games, but also about real investments, as we already mentioned for Cryptokitties, since the cryptocurrencies needed for purchases are nothing but a conversion of our Euros, Dollars, Pounds, or whatever fiat currency you use. Obviously, you can then resell your lands, your accessories, and your various NFT properties, and they may have increased their value with the changes you made to them. This is the reason why we speak of investments.

On metaverse, the focus is currently very high, just as much as it is for NFTs. It is expected that we will move more and more to 3D virtual worlds in the near future, where we will spend most of our time like in the movie "Ready Player One".

With Facebook changing the name of the company to Meta, a trigger is literally being pulled to race in this direction, with many investors who are stockpiling virtual land in the various metaverses, hoping to reap the benefits when this not too distant future will arrive.

We are still in the realm of speculation, and only time will give us the definitive answer as to the role of this technology in the near future, but Meta released news of great impact just before I was ready to publish this guide. Very soon we will be able to show our NFT collection on Instagram, and soon after that, the platform will allow us to trade, buy, and sell NFTs. We are all aware of the proportion of the impact that Facebook, Instagram, and Meta, in general, have on the life of each one of us. That near future seems just around the corner. Are you ready for it?

Are NFTs The Right Investment For You?

We've largely defined that the concept of NFT is relatively new and we're not yet clear on how it will move in the future, nor what paths it will open up within the digital economy.

It makes absolute sense for artists to turn their art into digital and have their pieces become NFTs.

The discourse, however, is much broader if you want to buy them for their collectible value. This is a highly speculative investment because it is almost impossible to predict the value of an NFT, as the price is influenced by the demand for the piece itself.

There are no established criteria that tell us with certainty when an NFT art project is appreciated and when it is not, so it is difficult to identify with certainty in advance a winning project. We can try to identify the most interesting projects, but only the future will tell if the investment will bring a profit. We have talked about many projects that were originally worth a few dollars and were then resold for large sums of money, for example, the aforementioned CryptoPunks that were originally given away for free and then resold for quite large sums of money, making them a highly profitable investment.

If you like to collect things and show your collections to people. If you already do it at some level, if you like to have beautiful and rare things, if you like to own expressions of creativity, then you might consider going into the world of NFT collecting. The factors that in my opinion you should take into consideration before deciding which purchase to make are the following:

- Who created the NFT
- What is the level of uniqueness of the NFT you intend to buy
- If it has been previously owned by others, to evaluate its demand

Analyze these factors to sort out the best options from the unattractive ones.

Although NFTs are attractive, are on everyone's lips at the moment, look set to grow in the future, and there is a lot of interest in joining the trend, I advise extreme caution.

Unfortunately, there is no way to know if it is simply a "bubble". Bubbles are always recognized after they happen, as has happened countless times in the investment world. So, there are no guarantees that NFTs bought today will be worth anything in the future. Consider all the risks you are facing very carefully before taking any action.

We opened this chapter by mentioning that NFTs are a new frontier of technology that is taking its first steps in its early stages. Always keep in mind that there are always numerous dangers when investing in the preliminary stages of new movements. You have to study, analyze, decide thoughtfully and cautiously, diversify your investments and consider the risk of investing at such a speculative level.

Before making any purchase in the NFT market you should conduct thorough research, and understand what you are investing your money in because there is no certain way to know where the market will go in the next few years. Right now it's a thriving market that's expanding fast, but there's no guarantee that it will continue to do so in the future. There are plenty of signs that make us believe that the actual trend will continue in the future, there are even signs that make us think that in the future the NFT market will grow bigger, but nothing is certain when we talk about investing. It is certainly an incredible market right now for generating revenue, but it is not without risk. Many people have indeed made millions of dollars from NFTs, but keep in mind that this is not always the case. We have already discussed the fundamental elements that play their role in these staggering figures. However, it is undeniable that NFTs are currently a good source of income for many categories of people, perhaps on a more modest scale than millions, but still interesting figures.

In assessing whether it is the right investment for you, you must also consider the risks of fraud. Of course, you can avoid most frauds by carefully choosing a reliable marketplace to operate on, but there have been many reported incidents where cryptocurrencies and NFTs have disappeared from the wallets of their users. So, you have to consider that you will have to pay a lot of attention to the security and protection of your digital wallets: dual authentication factors, really secure passwords, secret phrases with a very high level of security and their copy kept in very safe places, you also have to consider secure offline storage on cold wallets. We will discuss this in more detail in a further chapter on this guide, but it is something to consider when evaluating whether it is a good investment for you.

How To Buy NFTs

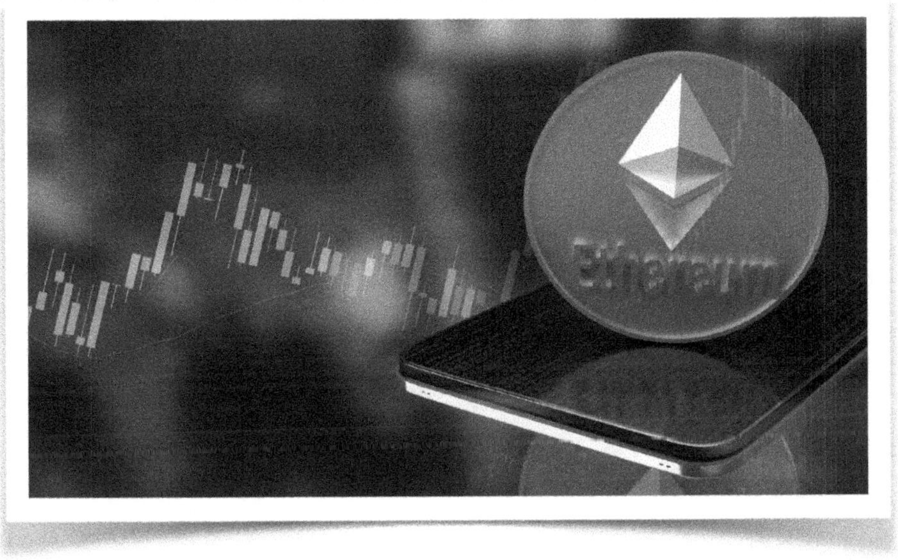

Now that we have analyzed the various types of NFT projects, and reasoned whether or not they can be a good type of investment for you, let's concentrate on understanding how to buy them and where to keep them.

To understand how to buy NFTs, we must first remember that we move in the world of cryptocurrencies, and it is only with this virtual money that you can make such purchases. The main cryptocurrency when we deal with NFTs is Ethereum, and to keep things as easy as possible we will concentrate our attention on it.

Now, I will explain the various steps of the purchase process starting with the fiat currency (i.e. the money you spend every day), its conversion into cryptocurrency, the actual buying process, and, finally, where the NFT you purchase is stored.

First, I'll list the steps and then we'll discuss them individually in more detail:

1. Open an account on a crypto exchange (this is where you purchase cryptocurrencies), then connect it to your bank account or to a bank card

2. Open a wallet where you can transfer cryptocurrencies and from which you can make purchases/store NFTs

3. Choose the marketplace that best suits your purchasing needs, then open an account on the marketplace, and connect your wallet to the account you just opened

4. Choose the NFT you want to buy, and make the purchase

5. Wait for the Gas Fee calculation, and then make the payment

6. Voilà! Now the NFT is yours, and it's well stored in your wallet

7. Keep your wallet safe and consider the possibility of moving your purchases to a special offline external storage device

As you can see, the steps are not very complicated, but if you are a total beginner in this world you might find this extra information useful.

1. The crypto exchange is where you buy cryptocurrencies to spend in exchange for your NFTs. There are many to choose from, the one considered most reliable and secure at the time of writing this book is Coinbase, which also has a very easy-to-use interface. If you are an investor in other areas, Etoro also gives you the possibility to buy cryptocurrencies but does not allow you to move any amount on the wallet, it imposes a minimum and this, for those who are just starting out and have limited funds, could be a problem. The main criterion to choose an exchange is its level of security and reliability, the cost of commission on transactions, and if you are a beginner, the ease of use of the app and its interface. NFTs are produced and sold in different cryptocurrencies, the prevalent one being Ethereum. Since you're just starting out, it might be easier to start here and then explore NFTs in different currencies. So, once you choose the exchange, you will have to create your profile, link it to a credit card or bank account and then buy the cryptocurrency, in our case

Ethereum. You'll have to convert Euros, Dollars, or Pounds, whatever fiat currency you use, into Ethereum.

2. A wallet is what allows you to make transactions with cryptocurrencies, whether they are sent to other people or used to purchase NFTs. The two main wallets at the moment are Coinbase Wallet and MetaMask. The choice of wallet should also be made in light of the purchases you intend to make because not all marketplaces accept all wallets. For example, OpenSea accepts both Coinbase Wallet and MetaMask, while Mintable only accepts MetaMask. Be careful when setting up the wallet because instead of the usual password you are used to, you are given a passphrase, which is a list of 12 words to remember in exact order. This passphrase is vital because it is not recoverable in any way if lost and without it, you lose every kind of access to your wallet and everything it contains both currencies and NFTs. Once the wallet is activated you just have to follow the simple on-screen instructions to move the Ethereum purchased on the exchange to the wallet. If you're using a smartphone you can do everything through the app, but if you're using a computer you'll need browser extensions to use some wallets, like MetaMask, for example.

3. In the section titled “Where to buy NFTs" we have extensively discussed the various marketplaces, you can start

to poke around and take a look at what they have to offer, and when you have made your choice, register to your favorite one. OpenSea is a great option to start looking at, both for the wide range of projects available for all budgets and for the ease and versatility of use, which in the early stages of something new is always a useful characteristic. During the registration phase, the chosen marketplace will make you follow a series of steps to associate your wallet to your account on the marketplace itself so that you will be able to make purchases.

4. Once you have created your account on the marketplace and hooked up a wallet with funds, you can start looking for your NFT and when you are ready you can click buy. Keep in mind that not all the NFTs you will see are available for sale, some of them may be on auction, and others may be owned by somebody else and you should make an offer in case the person is interested in selling. So you have two options: you can participate in the auction or make an offer to the owner if that suits you as a type of purchase, or you can search the filters in the chosen marketplace and set the filters to only show the NFTs actually for sale.

5. When the purchase of the NFT will be processed and before the sale is completed you will be charged the so-called Gas Fees, a cost in Ethereum usually a percentage of the

purchase cost of the NFT. It is a kind of management cost of the operation and the purchase will be completed only when you have accepted the price including the Gas Fees. It is a cost that many people don't like and many projects are trying to bypass it, but for the moment it is necessary if you buy NFTs on Ethereum. As I explained before, there are NFT projects based on cryptocurrencies other than Ethereum where the purchase does not include Gas Fees, it's up to you to decide if you want to start with these cheaper, but less popular options, or if you want to spend a little bit more to enter the largest and more popular market. Once the purchase is confirmed, the funds will be removed from your wallet and transferred to the wallet of the person who sold the NFT, and the NFT will do the reverse path, i.e. it will be transferred to your wallet.

6. At this point, you are the lucky owner of the NFT you chose and you should see it in your wallet in the NFT section.

7. If you are starting to invest in NFTs and your idea is to accumulate them because you like to keep them, or because you hope for a future increase in their value, I suggest you take extreme care of your wallet and its security. You may also want to consider not keeping all your NFTs in an online wallet. There are special external storage systems for cryptocurrencies and NFTs for sale. They look like USB keys

or small external HDs, and the most functional ones have a tiny screen and a Bluetooth transfer option. You need to create wallets in them, following the instructions included with the product when you purchase it, where you can transfer your NFTs and store them offline inside this small flash drive, which you can keep wherever you feel is safest. The most popular of these systems at this moment is Ledger, which is considered the safest and best performing, with the best option being Ledger Nano X (it's not the cheapest, but it's the best option if considering the rapport cost-performance). Anyway, you can find a wide range of other products on the market with similar specifics, so just pick the one you think serves better your purpose.

This is the simple step-by-step process to get you started with your first NFT. At first, it might seem a bit complicated, at least the first time because you will have to set up and then connect all the various tools you need. Just try a few times and you will see that you can do it without problems. Once the mechanism is set in motion, then, everything will be easier. In fact, you just need to keep your wallet always loaded with Ethereum and access the marketplace to make your purchases without difficulty. The pairing process between the wallet and the marketplace is done only once when you register for the first. After that, you only need to log in and buy, just like on any other platform where you shop.

Create And Sell NFTs

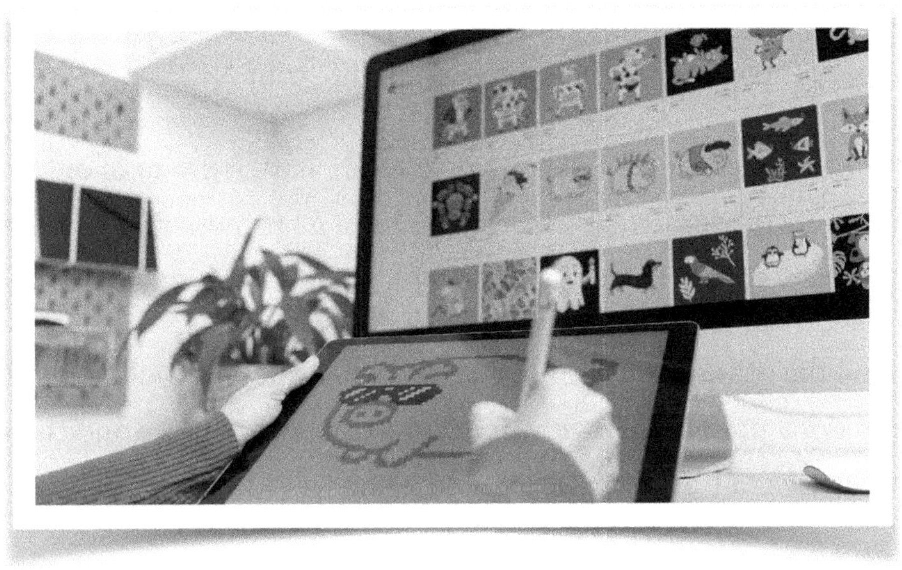

Now let's have a look at how to create and sell your own NFTs. Towards the end of the chapter, I will also discuss how to sell an NFT you didn't create but previously bought from somebody else.

First of all, I would like to discuss the creation criteria beyond an NFT, then the step-by-step process to do it.

Technically creating an NFT is a fairly simple process. You can decide to create an NFT for personal or commercial purposes.

If the purpose is commercial, if you want to sell them to make some money, there are a few considerations you should make. In the first place, you have to take into account that, despite the hype, people need to have a reason to buy your NFT.

If you are already an artist, if you already have a group of online followers for some reason, or if you have a business that you can somehow couple to the NFT concept, you are well on your way.

If, on the other hand, you're starting from scratch, you'll need to think of a project that will appeal to a certain audience and then advertise your project out there in some way.

If you're a digital artist, you already have your artwork ready and all you have to do is mint it into NFT. If you're a physical artist, you'll need to create a digital version of your artwork before minting it into an NFT. This could be a photo or a scan of your artwork, in the case of 3D art a video, or a GIF. In both cases, you should already have your own audience and collectors to present your project to, and these people should be potentially already interested in buying what you have to offer.

Usually, artists don't like the idea of digitalizing their art because they fear that other people will exploit their work and make money from it without their permission. But therein lies the huge difference in turning artworks into NFTs that we've discussed so far.

NFTs are for all intents and purposes digital certificates that, unlike replicable cryptocurrencies, have a unique identity and cannot be easily copied or reproduced. This allows artists to sell their work without the constant fear of being copied.

NFTs are also a great opportunity for influencers, Youtubers, and info business owners. These groups, usually, already have a vast group of followers on the various social media outlets, and if launching a project, they would already have an audience and good visibility as in the case of artists. I've seen some of them move in a very similar way: they've created a series of cute little collectible images in NFT format with bonuses and privileges attached. Essentially, the owners of the collectible images become part of a community more prominently. Some have access to private chats and Discord groups, others to courses and masterminds. This makes the buyer feel he has a special bond with the person who sold him the NFT. This sort of privileged relationship, which confers social status, is the main reason for buying, the reason is not the collectible image itself.

This is also the pattern to follow for those starting from scratch. You have to give the person a reason to buy. So, before you start, sit down for a moment and write down a plan. What do you have to offer? Surely, you know how to do something that someone might be interested in learning. Create your own digital image, create a community where you can teach or share experiences on that certain topic you chose, turn the project into an NFT project, and then advertise it on social media to sell it.

The good news is that the technical part of NFT creation is so simple that even beginners in the field can do it without any problem. The hard part is to create a project interesting enough to make people want to buy from you.

Let's take a look at the step-by-step creation and selling procedure. Then we will analyze each individual step to make things clearer, just as we did in the previous chapter. You'll notice that some steps are the same as the buying process because you'll need the same payment tools that you use to buy and in this case, you'll also use them to receive payments. Also, the marketplaces are the same. So, if you've already taken the first steps to set up the buying process, you won't need to do the setup phase again.

1. Open an account on a crypto exchange where you can buy cryptocurrencies and connect the exchange account to your bank account or to your credit card

2. Open a wallet where you can transfer the cryptocurrencies you've purchased, store the NFTs you don't want to sell, and receive payments

3. Choose the marketplace that best suits your needs

4. Create your own collection of digital art pieces

5. Turn your collection into digital tokens (NFT)

6. Put your NFT digital masterpieces on sale

7. Promote your works on your social channels

Let's add a few words about the different steps.

1. If you have already opened an account on the crypto exchange, you won't have to repeat this step. If you haven't done it yet, read the selection criteria listed in the previous chapter titled "How to buy NFTs". You will need this account to store the crypto you earn so you don't have to leave them all in the wallet, but you will also need it to fund your wallet when needed because you have to pay Gas Fees when you mint an NFT, same as when you do a purchase. If you don't know what I'm talking about, absolutely go back and re-read the previous chapter.

2. If you have already opened a wallet to purchase NFTs, you can skip this point, as the wallet is just one and you use it for every kind of transaction. When selling, the wallet will be used to receive payments for the works sold and to pay the Gas Fee necessary to mint your NFT.

3. The choice of the marketplace is important and delicate in the selling phase, maybe even more than in the buying phase. You will have to understand which platform is the best to show your project and sell the kind of art you have created. However, this is not the only criterion. Your initial budget can also be a determining factor in your choice. Some marketplaces give the possibility to create NFTs for free without an initial Gas Fee and this can be the best option for those artists who start with a very limited budget. OpenSea is the largest, most visited, and most money-moving marketplace, so it might be the right choice for the artist looking for visibility. Mintable offers the possibility to create Gasless NFTs, so it could be the right choice for the artist starting with zero budget. So, choose the marketplace that best suits your needs, register, and connect your wallet to your account on the marketplace. If you've already done this procedure for purchasing and the marketplace you are using to mint your NFTs is the same, just go on to the next step.

4. At this point, it is time to put together your collection of pieces to present to the market. We discussed the decision criteria at length at the beginning of this chapter. Create something that people want and give them a good reason to buy it. At this stage, all you need to do is have a nice folder of digital files that you will turn into NFTs in the next stage.

JPEG photos, animated GIFs, MP3 music. The limit here is your imagination.

5. Once you have decided on your collection you will have to transform each piece into an NFT. It's time to mint. To do so, just go to the appropriate section of the marketplace you have chosen. Usually, the page in your account says "Mint" or "Create", depending on the marketplace you are using, and it's well visible. You have to upload one file at a time. In addition to uploading the file that you are going to mint into an NFT, you will have to insert some important information regarding your artwork. That information is fundamental in order to sell your piece. You'll have to give a title and subtitle to your work, then put it in the right category and subcategory (for example category Art and subcategory Photography). You have to enter a description of the artwork you are uploading and then insert some #TAGS. You are also asked to decide if you give the copyright of the artwork to the buyer and if you give him the chance to resell it. Since the largest part of the NFT market currently speaks English, it would be ideal to write everything in English even if you come from a different native language. If you don't think you're up to it, you'll certainly find someone who can help you out with translations. Also, take into account the sales copy, that is, try to write in a persuasive way to increase sales, maybe read some books on the subject to find ideas

that can help you out to write a better description. Better description means a description with more chances to sell including, for example, the level of uniqueness of your piece or any other detail that your audience could find important when deciding if to buy or not. Also make the most of #TAGs by using highly searched words, but always in some way relevant to the work you are selling. Once you've filled in all the requested spaces and you have expressed your choices about sales and copyrights, start the minting of your NFT, so your file will be registered on the blockchain. Once the registration is completed your digital file has become an NFT. You'll need to affix some digital signatures via your wallet and pay Gas Fees (unless you've chosen a Gasless option) to complete the process.

6. When your works are all converted to NFTs you will see them in the section of your account in the marketplace that contains all your NFTs. Under each one, you'll find at least 2 action buttons. One button asks you if you want to put the NFT up for sale and the other if you want to pass it on to another person. When you click on the sell option, you will find 3 options (this is valid for most of the marketplaces). Option one is “sell now”. You set the price you want to get for your artwork in Ethereum and the work will be put on sale immediately. Option Two is “auction”. You’ll have to choose the duration in days or hours and the minimum in

Ethereum you're willing to accept and your work will be auctioned and sold to the highest bidder in the time you set. Option three is a hybrid “auction with an immediate sale”. You'll need to set your requirements as you would for the auction, adding an amount in Ethereum that you're willing to accept to sell immediately and skip the auction. Obviously, the best way to sell for you depends on many factors. The first one of which is your marketing strategy. For example, if you're already an artist with a good following the auction could create the right hype among your buyers, whilst if you're just getting known and you don’t already have a great follow, maybe you could consider other options or strategies. Some marketplaces also allow you to create one or more stores where you can group your work by collection or product type. Every store needs Gas Fees for its creation because each store is registered on the blockchain just like an NFT and you pay for each registration that takes place on the Ethereum blockchain. Related to this, I haven't found any marketplace that has a free option to create a shop. Certainly, having one or more stores can be useful, especially for the purpose of social proof, but you could easily start without one. Probably, you should first try to figure out if this art form is suitable for you and then eventually decide if you want to set up a virtual store and how much money to invest in your production and sale of NFTs.

7. Social media are the best channels to promote the trends of the moment and I would say that, at the moment, NFTs have fully earned this role. If you don't already have social media channels where you can promote your NFTs you have to create your accounts right away. Choose your favorite social media outlets and then use those channels to show your NFT artworks, and get customers to buy. You'll be able to link your social accounts to the marketplace, to ensure social proof, which is always very useful for sales. To get started, you may have to use a little money to create your first audience. Gradually, you will start to generate organic followers. If you already have some followers, try to involve them as much as possible and direct them to your works on the marketplace. For more established artists, using paid social media could be a solution to sell a lot more. It might be useful to contact a specialist in the field to save time and money and to get help to make the most of both organic and paid social.

To conclude the section on the creation and sale of NFTs I would like to discuss a legal issue, the is copyright. If you have had a look at the marketplaces whilst reading this book to start getting familiar with it, you will have noticed NFTs created by users who actually do not own the copyright of that content. I'm talking about movie clips featuring famous people or music they don't own the rights to use, rather than artwork created with characters clearly not owned by the creator and popularly known to be copyrighted. As much as these digital elements are widely available on the web and as much as it can be easier to sell this kind of NFTs, it is not possible to create and sell NFTs with copyrighted elements. There have already been many cases of NFTs being removed from sale on various marketplaces because of copyright infringement (i.e. abusive use of sounds, images, videos, etc.).

Pay close attention to this aspect and create NFTs only with artistic material that you actually own. Many sites are actively encouraging the public to create NFTs with any content, even if it doesn't belong to them, but you'll notice that the more serious marketplaces do a verification process before acquiring and registering your NFT on the blockchain. I reckon that this verification process is a clear sign of a more serious way of managing this industry. Also, keep in mind that in the boom phase that NFTs are experiencing now, the focus on copyright is very high to avoid abuse. If an artist should authorize you to use their material, be sure to obtain and retain a legally valid written statement. Unfortunately, there have been many cases in the history of people publicly stating that they didn't mind if someone used material they owned, only to launch copyright infringement suits a few years later against those who had relied on the previous statement.

It is also possible to sell NFTs that you did not create, but that you bought with a resale option. The procedure is the same described in step 6 of this chapter. If you have stored the NFT you want to sell in the marketplace itself, the procedure is exactly the same. If it's stored in your wallet or in your cold wallet (the offline option) it is enough that you make it visible in the section of your NFTs inside the marketplace you are using and then you can follow the selling procedure of step 6.

Transactions take place in real-time on the blockchain, so at the moment of the sale, you will see your NFT "disappear" from your account because it will be transferred immediately to the buyer. Exactly at the same time, inside your wallet will "appear" the equivalent of its value in Ethereum. It is a process that gets written on the blockchain exactly the moment it happens and has no margin of error. The new owner is registered on the blockchain and in the main time the old owner receives the payment.

We addressed the security situation in the previous chapter, i.e. storing your assets in the safest way possible. As you sell your works and start to make money, you should move a part of the earnings from your wallet to the exchange or, even better, to a cold wallet. Leaving all purchases and creations stored online involves various risks, in case your account is hacked. If you buy a lot of NFTs for investment, you should consider keeping them in a safe place until you decide to resell them. I reiterate the advice to buy a suitable external storage device. There are many brands, the best known at the moment is the one called Ledger as I mentioned in the previous chapter. This device is easily available on Amazon, just as are all the similar products meant to keep your cryptos safe. Following the instructions inside the product package, you can move on these external drives all the NFTs and cryptocurrencies you want to keep safe. At the time of purchase just make sure you choose a product that has an adequate capacity for your needs, in fact, many of the cheaper versions have very small capacities, which are fine for beginners who want to safely store their digital currencies but are not large enough for NFTs, or for too many different cryptocurrencies.

Why Have NFTs Reached Popularity Now?

I get this question asked often, and while there's no certain answer, there are a few indicators that can foreshadow the causes.

First of all, the pandemic has greatly changed the way people shop, bringing a lot more people online. People who didn't know how to buy online before are now getting by. So, NFTs have arrived in a wider market. They have also arrived in a market of people who were bored and had more money to spend, again because of the various lock-downs due to the virus.

Many people have been locked in their homes for months without being able to leave. So, why not buy a nice music album with some rarities in NFT format to listen to during those long days? And how about some very funny video clips?

All these people who have been locked up in their homes have also found themselves with a little extra money as they didn't have to pay for transportation to go to work or the meals they usually have to buy when they work.

In addition to these factors, cryptocurrencies have become very popular, more and more known, and understood by new segments of the population that only a few years ago were completely unaware of their existence.

All these facts in conjunction have definitely favored the understanding of NFTs and the growing curiosity towards this new phenomenon.

Why Do NFTs Cost So Much?

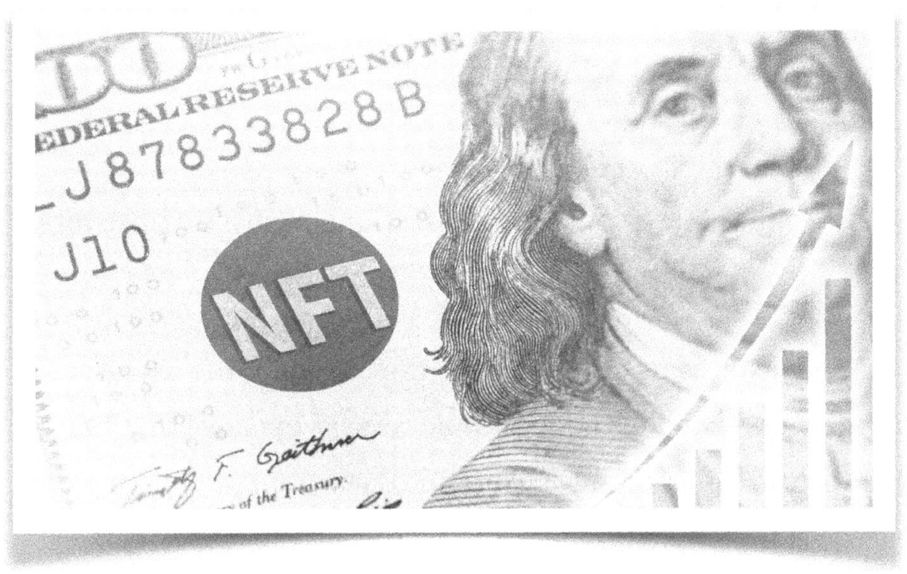

This is definitely the second question I get most frequently asked. The answer is easy to guess, considering what we have discussed so far.

Based on their uniqueness NFTs, or rather their possession, guarantee a certain social status. When you look with admiration at the millionaire portfolio of some investors in addition to the economic value spent, you are looking at the connections you establish with VIPs and celebrities, at the exclusive communities they have gained access to, at the musical or visual rarities that are their exclusive prerogative. So, the answer is that the high cost is justified by the uniqueness NFTs hold and by the social status they confer. NFTs have thrown us into a technological revolution that somehow makes us want to own rare and valuable items without having to worry about buying an illegal copy.

In my opinion, though, the real question is: why are investors willing to spend so much?

The social status usually interests the collector, the investor more is interested in the economic return. I believe that many investors are paying the astronomical sums often demanded based on their belief in increased value and profitability over time. We have already discussed the fact that this phenomenon is still too new to make true predictions, only time will show us if investors have been right.

Certainly, a good investment has been made by those who have invested in the creation of marketplaces where people can buy and sell NFTs and by those who create winning projects. The hype of the moment and the buying frenzy have undoubtedly produced substantial gains for these two categories of investors.

A final factor to take into consideration is that not all NFTs cost "a lot". Certainly, the highest-priced are those linked to the most interesting projects, but the record sales that are displayed on the news pages, many of which we have encountered in the previous chapters, are a bit of an exception. As with all areas of people's interest, the NFT topic also has peaks of interest that then wane. Record sales usually occur during the peaks, and then align and become more consistent during periods when interest wanes.

This last consideration may also be useful to you when deciding whether or not to purchase your first NFT. Are you at a market peak? Could you buy at a better price by waiting a few months when people's interest is elsewhere?

Often this incredible world of NFTs seems too good to be true and this scares a bit, it generates a fear of a crash that would take all investors with it. Unfortunately, we don't have a crystal ball, so we will have to reflect and evaluate seriously, as for any other investment, trying not to be influenced by those first multi-million dollar projects that caused the hype of this market.

In this analysis that I invite you to do, try to carefully separate the objective value from the subjective one, which could be the main misleading element.

People, you, me, anyone, attribute a certain value to a certain object, but if you were to ask a group of people the value of that object for them, you would get a different answer from every single person in that group. For someone, a luxury sports car would be the most valuable object, for someone else would be a rare designer handbag, for another one could be a dream vacation in a fabulous resort. The common element in all these answers is desire. If you have an intrinsic desire for something, you tend to consider that thing of very high value to you. It's the desire that creates a subjective value of a certain thing.

Satisfying a desire gives us pleasure, and people are always looking for pleasure, this is why we try to satisfy our desires. We can therefore say that subjective value is the value that each person is willing to assign to a certain object. It is an arbitrary value that can vary over time or as the person changes. When you really want something a lot, you are willing to pay exponentially more than what would be considered normal.

What does this make you think about? How much is an NFT really worth? Is its value subjective or objective? Do those who pay so much believe in its real value or are they subdued by the hype created? Maybe the hype around the topic is generating a desire in people that pushes them to pay much more than what would be considered normal.

It is certainly true that giving an objective value to objects is almost impossible, the price is always and in any case influenced by subjective elements: the season, the demand, how it satisfies the needs. With this digression, however, I just wanted to offer some serious food for thought to those who approach this field intending to invest. This is not at all meant to discourage those approaching this world. I'm always in favor of embracing new things, especially innovation, and technology. I just want to give food for thought so that those who decide to approach this world can do so with awareness, and not blinded by the glow of which the hype of the moment is always cloaked.

NFTs Pros And Cons

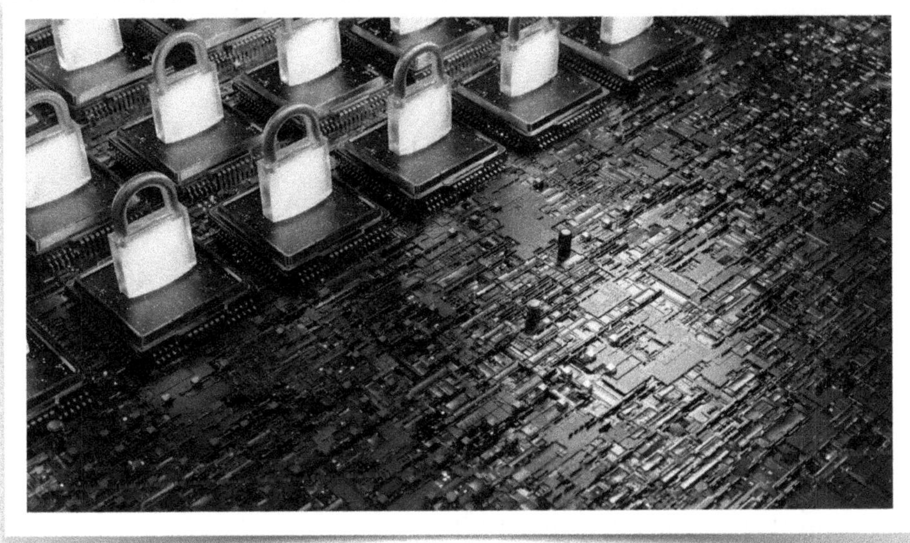

Let's start with the cons:

- It is a very young and immature current, with no precedents such that we can predict with a fair degree of certainty the direction it will take.

- The economic successes of many artists and creators have led to the creation of works that are worthless projects, created for the sole purpose of gaining a profit in a moment of hype, without giving any value to the buyer.

- The economic successes of some have led to the creation of numerous scams where works were sold as belonging to certain artists and creators, when in fact the NFTs were the work of the scammer.

- NFTs attract both collectors and cryptocurrency enthusiasts, this has generated a race to buy the most interesting projects at any price, with the risk of creating a "bubble".

- NFTs are not eco-friendly, in fact, the energy costs in terms of electricity that the blockchain requires for its maintenance, are quite high.

These are not scary cons and you can somehow protect yourself from all of them by using common sense and understanding before getting into this current and start investing in it. As far as eco-sustainability is concerned, on the other hand, solutions are already being sought by various marketplaces that aim to reduce this consumption to eliminate further doubt that this phenomenon has raised.

Let's come to the pros:

- Their uniqueness and certified ownership.

- NFTs have made it possible for digital artists to earn big money.
- NFTs can be resold to generate profit.
- NFTs make many procedures, such as auctions or sales, easy because they eliminate the need for middlemen.
- The NFTs enjoy all the benefits of the blockchain: decentralization, disintermediation and registration on an immutable ledger where content, movements, and transfers can be tracked and verified.
- The application fields of NFTs are more or less infinite, allowing future implementations in many types of business.
- NFTs have minimal costs for creation and virtually unlimited earnings for both individuals and companies.

The list of plus points is certainly full of important elements that will shape the future of NFT.

A Glimpse Into The Future

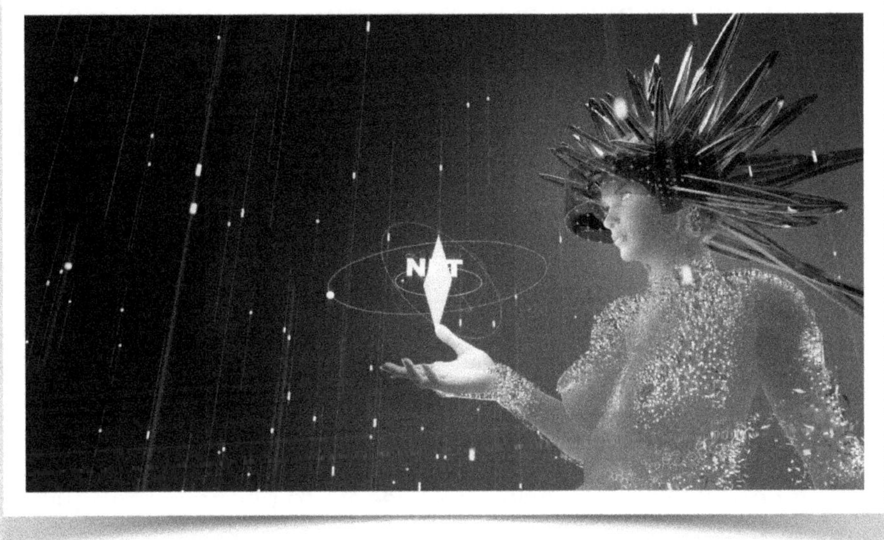

Human beings, their world, and technology have always evolved together, but we have reached a stage where the speed of evolution of technology exceeds any speed previously achieved.

Innovations have often led to consequences that were impossible to anticipate, and this is true of all great innovations. The inventors of the laptop certainly didn't expect that it would become impossible to get away from work because of their device with people taking it to bed to read emails. They also didn't expect the revolution they brought the world of work by creating millions of laptop lifestylers who work whilst traveling around the world. They only expected to improve the quality of work for a certain group of people.

We are now approaching a new era of futuristic technological advancements and each of us, through our own choices, is called upon to reshape our society and the entire world. We are only in the beginning stages of this revolution, but we must decide now what we want the world to look like because this will certainly determine the fate of human civilization and the direction that the human race will take.

NFTs seem to have evolved into a true audiovisual art form that is gaining control of the market and seems to be more than just a temporary craze. In fact, many museums and auction houses have already recognized NFTs as a new art form.

Metaverse and virtual experiences are just beginning to explore the potential of NFTs, but they have such a wide range of applications that all businesses are just beginning to discover how to incorporate them and use them for their own profit.

There are already many large global companies that have begun to delve into the world of NFTs, among the largest we have Coca-Cola, Nike, Diesel, and Microsoft, just to name a few. For these giants, NFTs are the new frontier of marketing. They can reach their customers with unique gifts, digital vouchers, and exclusive tickets. Using these free NFT gifts, they can increase their brand visibility and they can also create brand awareness in the customer. Those customers will become loyal to the brand as they will see the value of their NFT unique gift item grow on the marketplace where they display their NFT collection. The expectation is that this phenomenon will bring with it a revolution in marketing, advertising, and customers' buying process. The huge changes will be similar to those that happened with the transition from word of mouth to online advertising with specific targets such as Facebooks ads with target audiences or Google keyword target ads.

NFTs seem destined to write the future of the metaverse, that of business, that of investors, that of artists, but also that of the social status of individuals. At the moment their collections are not so easy to show to the world, but many companies are working in this direction.

One project that really impressed me is Lazy.com, a project signed by Mark Cuban, already mentioned as the founder of the incredible marketplace Mintable. The project of Lazy.com is not only to create a gallery to put on display, but to be able to link this gallery anywhere you can insert a URL, for example in your social biographies, in the signatures of emails, on your CV, and so on.

Once you can link your signature with your rarities collection in NFT format, that will become your digital business card. The whole world will be able to see this exclusive, million-dollar business card and assess your social status accordingly. In case you don't have anything impressive to show, your social status will still be assessed accordingly. Evaluate by yourself all the possible implications.

The decisions that each of us will make from now on will certainly determine the evolution of the NFT and consequently the shape that our society and the world around us will take. Will we all find ourselves in the metaverse instead of the pub? Will it be in the metaverse that we will go to work in a few years? Will we move our businesses there? Instead of real clothes will we be buying their NFT representations to cloth our avatar? Or is it just a big bubble destined to disappear? What do you think? What would you like to happen?

Get ready for the future because it doesn't matter what direction it will take but it's just around the corner, in some cases, it's already here. I can't wait to see what will happen with NFTs on Instagram.

Conclusion

At this time, NFTs are still at an early stage of development. We cannot know for sure how they will evolve or how they will affect the world. What we do know and realize is that the world is moving more and more toward a decentralized economy and NFTs, being part of it, are a further push in that direction.

If we look around, it's easy to see that new companies are adopting cryptocurrencies and using blockchain systems daily. Today, you can buy a house in crypto and travel around the world paying for everything with your Bitcoins. Who knows what you'll be able to do tomorrow with your NFTs?

Thanks to the many apps and up-to-date payment systems that use blockchain technology you can already do a lot of things and many types of purchases with cryptocurrencies: you can buy a car or just pay for a coffee, or generate an NFT. When the number of people using these apps and payment systems will increase, we should start to have a clearer and more concrete vision of the direction NFTs will take and what their use will be focused on.

The world is changing faster and faster, and blockchain technology is making sure to make these changes even faster.

More and more people are adopting this technology for their own purposes, we just have to see where this will lead us and try to keep up with the change because everything is so fast it's easy to get left behind and get cut off.

The history of NFTs is still very recent and a bit tortuous, but just take a look at the multitude of projects and attempts to use them, and you can make a pretty accurate prediction of their absolutely exponential growth. Collectors are going crazy over this phenomenon. The market grows and implements NFTs in correspondence to the needs of buyers who then enjoy the fruits of their investment. What about you, what do you think?

I hope this book has helped you to get a clear idea of the much-talked-about NFT universe. I hope to have given you food for thought on this new method of investment and on its social as well as economic importance. I hope now you have enough elements to decide if it is an investment method that is somehow congenial to you or not, and that you have acquired all the necessary information to become part of it if you have so decided.

Finally, I hope I have kept my promise and that I have managed to explain this complicated universe to you in a simple enough way to be suitable for a beginner. I will be immensely pleased to know your honest opinion of what you have read in the pages of this book.

Thank you for staying with me till the end,

All the best

Alex

Crypto Academy

www.ingramcontent.com/pod-product-compliance
Ingram Content Group UK Ltd.
Pitfield, Milton Keynes, MK11 3LW, UK
UKHW020139250726
13967UKWH00002B/751